EFFECTIVE PRAYER

EFFECTIVE PRAYER

Ernest Holmes

Compiled and Edited by
WILLIS KINNEAR

Science of **Mind** Publishing
Los Angeles

Copyright ©1966 by Science of Mind Publishing

Originally Published: October 1966
This Printing: December 1995

Published by Science of Mind Publishing
3251 West Sixth Street,
P.O. Box 75127
Los Angeles, California 90075

Photo Credit: Garo Enjaian
Cover Design: Randall Friesen

All rights reserved—no part of this book may be
reproduced in any form without permission in writing
from the publisher, except in the case of brief quotations.

Printed in the United States of America
ISBN: 0-911336-02-8

CONTENTS

Introduction
Page 6

— Part One —
THE FOUNDATION

A basis for belief in and understanding of the nature of prayer

Page 9

— Part Two —
THE PRACTICE

Certain concepts and attitudes essential in making prayer a dynamic power

Page 19

— Part Three —
PRACTICAL SUGGESTIONS

A variety of ideas which may be used in making prayer more effective in your life

Page 33

INTRODUCTION

No longer is there any question or doubt but that prayer can change things. There is no aspect of life that it cannot affect. Through prayer, life can become a continuing experience of health, happiness, success, joy, and abundance.

Prayer is a very personal thing, a dialogue between man and his Maker. No person can tell another how to pray, any more than another can be told how he should always think. However, the question arises as to just what is involved in making prayer effective in a controlled manner.

It appears that there are certain requisites which are the basis for effective prayer. First of all, prayer has its foundation in one's religious beliefs. Certain religious convictions seem to be detrimental to prayers being answered, while others provide a basis for outstanding results.

The first part of this volume presents the personal beliefs of the great spiritual leader, the late Ernest Holmes. Through the years those who have come to believe as he did have found prayer to be a constant dynamic factor in their everyday living.

The second part presents ideas on how to use the power of prayer. At heart Dr. Holmes was a great teacher, and he here guides the reader into understanding of the nature of prayer and how to use it in an effective manner.

In the last part will be found a variety of practical suggestions for effective prayer, or spiritual mind treatment as Dr. Holmes termed it. The ideas brought forth here are aids which will enable the individual to have his prayers be more specific factors in his life. These are ideas which he presented in instructing a special class in creative prayer and they are presented in what might be termed outline form.

For those who are encountering the writings of Ernest Holmes for the first time, many consider him to be one of the outstanding religious-philosophers of our day. His great contribution was the development of the teaching known as Science of Mind. This presented and brought down to earth in plain language a philosophy of life that is intellectually sound and acceptable, as well as being emotionally satisfying.

Science of Mind Publications

PART ONE

THE FOUNDATION

Throughout the ages prayer has been an important factor in man's life. Regardless of different religious convictions or cultural backgrounds prayer has been found to be productive of results.

This would imply that there is some universal factor involved, although it has been interpreted in many ways. For prayer to consistently have the desired result seems to depend upon going behind the various interpretations, the superstitions involved, the dogma and ritual, and getting back to the basic factor itself.

To do this requires a certain degree of understanding of the nature of Life and man, an understanding that is based on the spiritual wisdom of the ages and at the same time incorporates the truth of the ever-advancing front of knowledge in today's world.

What I believe naturally divides itself into three parts: What I believe about God, what I believe about man, and what I believe about the relationship between God and man.

First, I believe that God is universal Spirit, and by Spirit I mean the Life-Essence of all that is, that subtle Intelligence which permeates all things and which, in man, is self-conscious mind. I believe that God is present in every place, conscious in every part, the Intelligence or Mind of all that is.

I believe that man is the direct representative of this Divine Presence on this plane of existence. Man is the most highly evolved intelligence of which we have any knowledge. Man, being the highest representation of God here, is more nearly like God than any other manifestation on earth.

I believe that the relationship between God and man, between the Infinite and the finite, is a direct one; and that the avenue through which the Mind of God expresses to the mind of man is through the mind of man himself. We have the ability to think, to know, to perceive, to receive, and to act. What

THE FOUNDATION

are these attributes other than a direct channel through which the universal Spirit flows to us?

I do not feel that we approach God through any formula, sacred prayer, or intermediary, but rather that the Spirit of God, the eternal Mind, is the Power by which we think and know. It is self-evident that the only God whom we can know is the only God whom we do know, and that this knowing is an interior process of our own belief and perception. We can know no God other than the God whom our consciousness perceives.

But, some will say, while it is true that we cannot think outside of ourselves, we can know that which is outside of ourselves, because we do know things that are not within us. This is true, as it is true that we have a city hall, but to me that city hall would have no existence unless I were first aware of the fact. It has no existence to those who never heard of it. This is true of everything; and, while the possibility of knowledge may and must expand, we cannot know that which we do not perceive.

Therefore, I feel that God is to each one what each is to God. The Divine nature must be, and is, infinite; but we can know only as much of this nature as we permit to flow through us. In no other way can God be known to us. I believe the relationship between God and man is hidden within, and that when we discover a new truth, or find out

EFFECTIVE PRAYER

something further about an old truth, it is really more of this infinite Mind revealing Itself through us.

I believe, then, in a direct communication between the Spirit of God and man—God personifying Himself through each and all. This is a beautiful as well as a logical concept, and an unavoidable conclusion. This makes of the human being a Divine being, a personification of the Infinite.

But if we are Divine beings, why is it that we appear to be so limited—so forlorn, poor, miserable, sick, and unhappy? The answer is that we are ignorant of our own nature, and also ignorant of God's Law which governs all things.

I believe that all things are governed by immutable and exact laws; these laws cannot be changed or violated. Our ignorance of any law will offer no excuse for its infringement and we are made to suffer, not because God wills it, but because we are ignorant of the truth. We are individuals and have free will and self-choice. We shall learn by experience about things mental and spiritual just as we do about things physical and material. There is no other way to learn, and God Himself could not provide any other way without contradicting His own nature.

But if everything is governed by Law, is there any spontaneous Mind in the universe? Yes, but this

THE FOUNDATION

spontaneous Mind, which is God, never contradicts Its own Nature; It never violates Its own Law. We shall cease to misuse the Law as we learn more about ourselves and our relationship to the Whole. Experience alone will do this for us. We are made free, and because we are made free we shall have to abide by our nature and gradually wake up to the truth of our being.

Since I believe that everything is governed by exact laws, I believe all that the scientific world teaches, provided it is true in theory and principle. But should anyone in the scientific world, realizing that all is governed by law, thereby exclude the necessity of a spontaneous Spirit pervading all things, I would ask him this question: By what power of intelligence do you recognize that all things are governed by exact laws? And he would be compelled to answer that he knew by the power of a spontaneous intelligence welling up within him.

We are living in a universe governed by mechanical laws which have no conscious intelligence or personal volition. Of this we are sure. But the very fact that we can make this declaration proves that we are not governed by mechanical law alone, for mechanical law cannot, by reason of its very nature, recognize itself. When we come to self-recognition we have already arrived at spontaneous self-knowingness.

EFFECTIVE PRAYER

We are subject to the Law of our being, but this Law is not a Law of bondage, but one of liberty—liberty under Law.

I can conceive of a spontaneous Spirit and an immutable Law; the Spirit, and the *way* It works. This position has been accepted by the great thinkers of every age. It is self-evident. Spirit can never contradict Itself. Neither can It violate Its creative action through Its own Law.

I believe that we are surrounded by a mental or spiritual Law—the Law of Mind—which receives the impress of our thought and acts upon it. This is the Law of all life and we may consciously use It for definite purposes. I am not superstitious about this Law any more than I would be about the laws of electricity or any other natural law, for nature is always natural.

God works through what we call the principle of evolution or unfoldment, and we are subject to the laws involved. It is not a limitation, but is the only way through which our freedom and individuality can be guaranteed to us. There is an unfolding principle within us which is ever carrying us forward to greater and greater expressions of life, in freedom, love, and joy.

Each one of us is, I feel, at a certain level of evolution, and on the pathway of an endless expression of Life, Truth, and Beauty. Behind us is the All,

THE FOUNDATION

before us is the All, and within, or expressing through us, is as much of this All as we are ready to receive. I believe absolutely in the immortality and the continuity of the individual stream of consciousness, which is what we mean by the individual life-stream. Humanity is an ascending principle of life, individuality, and expression through experience and unfoldment.

I do not believe in hell, the devil, damnation, or in any future state of punishment; or any other of the fantastic ideas which have been conceived in the minds of those who are either morbid or who have felt the need of a future state of damnation to which to consign the immortal souls of those who have not agreed with their absurd doctrines. God does not punish people. There is, however, a Law of Cause and Effect which governs all and which will automatically punish, impartially and impersonally, if we conflict with the fundamental Harmony. This is bad enough, but it seems to me to be necessary, else we could not learn. It is one thing to believe in hell and damnation and quite another proposition to believe in a Law which involves retribution.

The Law, with Its retributive action, maintains balance, compensation, and equilibrium which is necessary to the universe. As we sow we shall, no doubt, reap. But I am sure that full and complete salvation will come alike to all. Heaven and hell are states of

EFFECTIVE PRAYER

consciousness in which we now live, according to our own state of understanding. We need not worry about either reward or punishment, for both are certain. In the long run, all will be saved from themselves through their own discovery of their Divine nature, and this is the only salvation necessary and the only one that could really be.

I do not believe that there is anything in the universe which is against us but ourselves. Everything is and must be for us. The only God who exists, the "Ancient of Days," wishes us well, knows us only as perfect and complete. When we shall learn to know as God knows, we shall be saved from all mistakes and all troubles. This is heaven.

The apparent imperfection is but a temporary experience of the soul on the pathway of unfoldment. Man is a creature of time and of the night, but the day will break and the dawn of an everlasting morning of pure joy is in store for all. Meantime, God is with us and we need have no fear for He doeth all things well. I feel that we have reason to rejoice in what truth we now have, and that we may look toward the future in confident expectancy, with gratitude and certainty that as we gain greater understanding we shall receive greater illumination.

I believe in every man's religion for it is the avenue through which he worships God. I believe in my own religion more than in that of anyone else

THE FOUNDATION

because this is the avenue through which I worship God.

I believe in a religion of happiness and joy. There is too much depression and sorrow in the world; these things were never meant to be and have no real place in God's world of Love. Religion should be like the morning sun, sending forth its glorious rays of light; it should be like the gently falling dew covering all; like the cool of the evening and the repose of the night. It should be a spontaneous song of joy and not a funeral dirge. From the fullness of the heart the mouth should speak.

I believe in the Fatherhood of God, the brotherhood of man, and the bond of Unity that binds all together in One Perfect Whole. I believe that God speaks to us in the wind and the wave and proclaims His presence to us through all nature, but most completely through our own minds and in our hearts which proclaim His Life and Love.

There is no question about the creativeness of thought. However, if any thought is creative, it must follow that all thought is creative. The Law of Mind is exact, not capricious. The only question is: How are we going to use this creative Power within us?

Shall we use It consciously and constructively, and for definite purposes? Or, shall we use It unconsciously and more or less destructively, merely because we do not understand It?

The Science of Mind and its practice as spiritual mind treatment is the answer to this question.

E. H.

PART TWO

THE PRACTICE

To use prayer in a practical and effective manner certain things must be considered as necessary.

Some may believe that prayer must follow a formula, a certain ritual, which may be adequate for them. It has been found that for greater efficacy prayer needs to have more freedom of expression, a greater flexibility. For this reason it is felt that instead of prayer being a formula, there is a basic technique which may be followed by the individual and adapted to his own particular personality and need.

Here are presented ideas which have proved to be valid by all who have used them. People of all religious denominations have applied them in their prayer life and have discovered an entire new world of living open up.

WHAT THE GREAT, THE GOOD, AND THE WISE of all ages have taught, which is also the very foundation of modern psychology and science, is that the universe is a spiritual system. This does not deny the physical universe, that is a part of it.

So when we say that our body is a spiritual body we are not saying that we have no eyes, or we have no feet, or we have no stomach. These things are all included in the spiritual system. God's world is not a world of illusions but of realities. The illusion is not in the thing but in the way we look at it and think about it. Everything is as real as it is supposed to be.

We live in the physical universe, the nature of which appears to be, first of all, as though there were a Divine Presence, a universal Spirit, an infinite Person back of it. God as pure Spirit, as infinite Person, also is always personal to each one of us, always personified in us. The God that is everywhere is also in us.

There could be only goodness in the nature of God or God would be self-destructive. Plato said that

THE PRACTICE

God is goodness, truth, and beauty. A modern prophet said that God is life, truth, and love. They are both correct. God is the Essence of life, the Essence of intelligence, the Divine Presence everywhere present, and therefore at the center of our own being.

We are more than a reflection of God, we are more than an emanation or a projection of God; we are an attribute, an incarnation, an individualization. There is nothing else we could be. Naturally, as a result there is a pressure against us at all times to be like God: lovable, beautiful, joyous, whole, complete, satisfied.

We are not only surrounded by the Divine Presence, we are also immersed in the infinite Law, which has no warmth, no color. It is not a person, It is a Principle responding to us creatively by corresponding with our mental attitudes. We differentiate between God as the infinite Person, the Divine Presence, and the Law as the Divine Principle. One is the engineer and the other the engine.

There must be both, otherwise we could not have a complete cosmology or a complete philosophy of life. That God is infinite Person and is at the same time infinite Law is what physicist Sir James Jeans meant when he said that we can think of the universe as an infinite Thinker thinking mathematically. The infinite Thinker is the Person, and thought is mani-

EFFECTIVE PRAYER

fested through the Law of Its own nature. Everywhere we look we see that the universe is a combination of the Presence and the Law.

Certain fundamental principles do exist in the physical universe and they operate mechanically and mathematically. Similarly, we find that we are surrounded by and immersed in a Law of Mind, a creative medium which automatically acts upon or reacts to our every thought. Men like Emerson, known as one of the ten greatest intellects who ever lived, thought, and rightly we may be sure, that for every law of nature that we observe—such as those in chemistry and physics—we shall some day find a corresponding spiritual or mental law. That is why Emerson said that he believed in a law of parallels. This would mean that for every law that science discovers we will find a comparable spiritual one. This is why Dr. Alexis Carrel said that faith, without violating any physical law, uses another set of laws that transcend physical laws.

The Bible says: "And the earth was without form, and void; and darkness was upon the face of the deep. And the Spirit of God moved upon the face of the waters." All creation is the result of Divine Ideas going forth through Law into manifestation.

These ideas are the essence of what the great of the ages have always taught. It is all very simple, but one of our great troubles is that we mentally get

THE PRACTICE

uneasy when we think we are going to have to think. But thinking is the easiest thing in the world; however, we need to do it in a constructive manner.

We can interpret the teaching of Jesus as being built on the assumption, the theory, that there is *something* that reacts to our thought exactly as we think it. This is what creation is. The Word of God manifested in definite form. That which is created is not a cause, but it is an effect. We are one with the Creator and that which is created. We are in it, with it, like it, a part of it. We did not make it that way and we cannot change it. There is nothing we can do about it other than to accept it and utilize our position in it.

How shall we do this? How do we use any law? We use the laws of electricity consciously, simply, directly, and by personal choice. The laws of electricity have no volition. So it is with the use of the Law of Mind. We must use It with full awareness. But we must remember that the Law of Mind, or Spirit, which we may use consciously, will always return to us exactly what we are thinking. We cannot conceal anything. The Bible says: " . . . there is nothing covered, that shall not be revealed; and hid, that shall not be known." Shakespeare said: "This above all: to thine own self be true   And it must follow, as the night the day, / Thou canst not then be false to any man." Emerson said: "What you are stands

EFFECTIVE PRAYER

over you the while, and thunders so that I cannot hear what you say to the contrary."

We need to be fully aware that we cannot fool the Law of Cause and Effect; that thought becomes manifested. We can fool each other, and unfortunately we fool ourselves most of the time, but the Law of Mind is as a law of reflection returning to us the exact content of our thought.

This Law is not a physical law as such. It is comparable to the laws of science but applies to the realm of Mind and Spirit. It is a Law which responds to our word; that is, our thought, mental image, or idea. Everything that is must first exist in the Mind of God, or our mind, as an idea which is then projected into form.

In our lives we may find comparable situations in psychosomatic medicine which seeks to uncover mental causes for physical ailments. It finds patterns of thoughts, collections or clusters of thoughts, which are producing physical correspondents. Emotional strain and stress has been found to cause great physical repercussions. There is an invisible but adequate cause for every condition that exists in our lives.

We have much in our lives that we do not enjoy and we would like to get rid of. There is nothing wrong about using the Law of Mind for any good we desire providing it does not interfere with another

THE PRACTICE

person's good. We should always ask ourselves if what we wish produces harmony, and then be sure there is no hurt in it to anyone.

We can only come into the experience of harmony by thinking harmoniously. So no matter what we profess, what the lips say, it is out from the mind and heart that the experiences of life come. So to begin to constructively use the Law of Mind rests on the conversion of our consciousness. Our life on the outer is a reflection of the inner.

If God is in every place there can be no place where God is not. So in the midst of the storm there is a calm; in the center of every man's life is pure Spirit. But we can get back to It only by imbibing the nature of Its Being and the spirit of Its Nature; that is, by being like It. So we must change our thought patterns.

The creative nature of our thought involves the sum total of the content of our mind. This means that our habitual thought patterns are being reflected in all our images of thought. Also, the subconscious mind is a great creative reservoir. Then, we are all immersed in and experiencing the race consciousness, and it is operating through each one of us to a greater or lesser degree. Any negativity of thought we are aware of arising from such sources may be changed by consciously identifying ourselves with and maintaining only good positive ideas. Such

EFFECTIVE PRAYER

new identification thus becomes the law of our life.

If everything there is is the operation of Intelligence on or through Law, the Word of God upon the waters, then our every word is an idea which automatically has the seed of fulfillment in it. The idea is the seed that takes root in the Law of Mind, which in turn produces the results. Moses said: " . . . the word is . . . in thy mouth . . . " Every word you speak, every idea, whether positive or negative, is a creative factor. " . . . the Word was made flesh, and dwelt among us . . . . "

We do not change Reality. But our thoughts are like writings on a blackboard, they may be rubbed out and replaced by others. We must not only continuously identify ourselves with the desires of our heart, being certain they do not deny goodness, but must erase and remove all contrary ideas. Jesus indicated that God desires us to have every good thing. The song of a joyous life is always being sung but we do not hear it. But God cannot give us love through hate; God cannot give us peace through confusion; God cannot give us happiness through misery; God cannot give us joy through our tears. God cannot express harmony through discord. God cannot express in opposites. If He did He would destroy Himself, which He cannot do. Because of this Jesus said: "Ye cannot serve God and mammon." And in the *Bhagavad Gita* we find the admo-

THE PRACTICE

nition that we will have to do away with the pairs of opposites. We cannot walk east and west at the same time.

We have to learn that if we want to draw out of the Divine Nature that which is in It, we must co-operate with the nature of Its Being. That is the only limitation that is set on man. What we may believe about It will not change It. All the belief the world has ever had about hell never created any hell outside of the discord in the consciousness of the people who believed in it. There is no more chance that there is a hell than there is in the idea that God is the devil.

To experience goodness we will have to identify ourselves with goodness. That is not easy. For instance, we start the day by saying, "I am going to believe only in harmony." Then we see a headline in the paper, we listen to the radio, and talk with each other. Then we say, "Well, harmony is in God —heaven. I wish it were here on earth." In this way we separate ourselves from it. We should not only refuse to comment on the discord, but we should not even dare to hold it in our thought. To think about a thing is to will to do it, and to have the will to do it is to bring it about in our lives.

We will have to learn to think straight. What does this mean in actual practice? For example, we will take the case of a person who thinks he has no

EFFECTIVE PRAYER

friends. Loneliness is one of the greatest diseases in the world; a sense of aloneness, of not belonging to the universe, a sense that no one cares. More people suffer from this than from anything else, and it produces a larger percentage of suffering than all other diseases. We should instruct such a person to realize that:

"God is in you. God is in everyone else. There is One Mind common to all individuals. There is One Person. All people are in this One Person; every person is a personification of this One; therefore there is something in you that is one with every other person you will ever meet. Solve your problem by never again believing anything else. Identify yourself with that One in everyone you meet; know that everyone you meet is just a little different expression of that One, and meet them as that One and you will meet yourself in that One."

Everything is good up to now, very easy to understand, but what he is called on to do is hard. Perhaps the first time he goes out someone will say something unkind to him and he will say, "I don't see the One in that one." We should not condemn him but sympathize with him because we are talking about ourself. We only react to our own reactions. This person is hurt, feels badly inside. What is he going to do? Start all over again. Gradually the word which he affirms will happen to him through the action of the

THE PRACTICE

Law of Mind—a Law of Cause and Effect.

The subjective content of our mind is very much greater than we are consciously aware of. Not only is it our silent power of attraction and repulsion, but it represents the true polarity of the mind. However, there is nothing in it that was not put there, and what we put into it we can take out. But there must be a conversion, a catharsis, a purging of the negative subjective emotional content of our thought. Gradually, by identifying ourselves with love, happiness, friendship, and harmony, our thought patterns change and then we will encounter only situations which are like them, no matter where we go or whom we may meet. Emerson announced this when he said: "The only way to have a friend is to be one." Love everybody! We cannot afford the self-imposed ravages of hate.

Remember we are always working with an immutable Law, an unfailing Principle, an available Power. The one who does this will see the day when the desires of his heart will become the facts of his experience. This can be accomplished with any aspect of life, no matter what it is—love, success, or health.

The Law of Mind works as a law of identity, reproducing identically the content of our thought in and as our experience. It works by involution and evolution. We must get the ideas into the mind and

EFFECTIVE PRAYER

allow them to work out. But very frequently people do not realize this and do not give the Law a chance to work. It is like planting seeds in the garden and then tearing them out again before they come to fruition. We must watch the seeds of thought and cultivate them. We must separate the ideas with intelligence, separating the wheat from the chaff and saving the wheat. God always gives the increase if we trust in and rightly use the Law of His nature.

It is as simple as this: We are surrounded by an infinte Law that can do anything. There is no limit to It and It does not know anything about big and little. But what the Law does for us It must do through us. Therefore our problem is to convert our own thought. We must consciously and subjectively accept only that which we wish to experience.

We convert the mind by the audible or silent expression and acceptance of constructive words, thoughts, ideas, or beliefs. This is prayer, communion, realization, or meditation—whatever we choose to call it. Thus we automatically change our thought patterns through the Law of Cause and Effect. As our thinking rises to a higher comprehension of the nature of Spirit—the Source of health, beauty, love, life, and abundance—automatically our thought patterns are improved and become more productive of good in our lives.

We must imbibe and embody a sense of both the

THE PRACTICE

Divine Presence and the infinite Law. As we do so we may with surety affirm that our thoughts and ideas become more Divine-like in their nature. We need to be more concerned about getting our thought straightened out than about the results that will follow, for they will follow automatically as night the day.

For clearer thinking in what we call a spiritual mind treatment, effective prayer, we watch ourselves, and see that if in it we have placed any limitation relative to the past, present, or future which may limit the possibility of its complete fulfillment. If we have, we are automatically causing the Law to act through that limitation and not to act freely on the good that is desired. We are conditioning the action of the Law to what we have accepted—good or bad. Jesus stated the whole thing simply when he said: " . . . as thou hast believed, so be it done unto thee . . . ."

We must watch over our own thought carefully, painstakingly, patiently, and not become discouraged. Just as surely as we do this we are bound to have our prayers become effective in our experience. The one who successfully uses spiritual mind treatment is merely one who knows these things, practices them, and understands and believes them. Through experience one learns that when one does this the result will be certain for any person, situation, or

EFFECTIVE PRAYER

condition. The Spirit responds alike to everyone.

We may control our thinking, and this can be done if we will but do it. It does not matter what someone else thinks. The only thing that matters is this: that in the integrity of our own soul, the union of our own consciousness with God and the Universe, that thing which we demand of the Spirit within will happen, that good which we accept as ours will come to pass. And finally, sooner or later, every person who is awake and alive will know himself. He will come to self-awareness and that self-awareness will include a knowledge of his union with Life. He will become whole within himself. What a wonderful thing to contemplate!

We must always realize that we are in conscious partnership, now, with the Infinite, and the good word that goes forth from our mouth, even as the word of Jesus, is the Word of God. Then as that word demonstrates itself in our individual lives, everyone we meet whom we can help will ask for that help and we shall have demonstrated that which all the ages have passionately looked forward to.

PART THREE

PRACTICAL SUGGESTIONS

Everyone desires that his prayers be effective. Probably the most valuable aid today in this respect is the teaching and philosophy advanced by Science of Mind.

The following pages contain aids, suggestions, and vital ideas which relate to prayer for specific purposes. They can help you clarify your thinking so that it can be more creative and constructive.

However, they need to be interpreted in your own way, they need to be made yours, for only then do they add vitality to your prayers.

Effective prayer is both an art and a science; a thing of the heart and the intellect. With these ideas you can come to develop your prayer life to a point where it is a continuously creative factor for your daily joy of living.

It is certain that none of you receive as much benefit from your prayers or spiritual mind treatments as you might. You do not permit your consciousness to range in the field of greater possibilities. A certain time should be taken definitely each day for the enlargement of consciousness. This is done by reminding your imagination that the field with which it deals is limitless; that Mind is the creator and the sustainer; that Mind is infinite, ever available, and always responsive to you.

The basic principle upon which spiritual mind treatment rests is that there is creative power in thought; that Truth known is demonstrated, and that right ideas are manifested by the Law of Mind. The power to act resides in Spirit. The action of Spirit is the movement of consciousness. Your understanding of this, your comprehension of spiritual Power, enables you to use the Law of Mind for specific purposes.

God manifests through man in his ideas. The idea is correct when you have a spiritual sense of it, when you substitute a consciousness of unity for a con-

PRACTICAL SUGGESTIONS

sciousness of separation. In other words, you are using the Principle correctly when you substitute spiritual ideas for objective facts and proceed upon the basis that new ideas create new facts.

Through the process of thought you may remove old and undesirable ideas, replacing them with new and more constructive ones which can then become a definite program for right action for you. The process of knowing that this is happening and declaring that right ideas are made known to you constitutes an important step in spiritual mind treatment.

You should forever increase this receptivity, continuously extend and expand your comprehension. You should declare a hundred times a day: "Good and more good is mine. An ever-increasing good is mine. There is no limit to the good which is mine. Everywhere I go I see this good, I feel it, I experience it. It presses itself against me, flows through me, expresses itself in me, and multiplies itself around me."

Your consciousness of good is acted upon by the Law of Mind. Such awareness acts as a law of elimination and expulsion to every discord, to every sense of accumulated bondage, to every sense of impure congestion or accumulation. Your prayer directs the Law and is the motivation of its power. Be sure you do not deny your own understanding.

EFFECTIVE PRAYER

The inertia of human thought, rising as it does from the morbidity of race consciousness and the mesmeric grip of race suggestion, seeks to claim that there is not in or through you the power to heal. Recognize this false argument for actually what it is. It is nothing claiming to be something. It is a lie claiming to be the truth. It is a habit of thought unwilling to surrender itself.

You must know that your prayer absolutely dispels and obliterates and shakes loose this mental inertia, and frees the consciousness to right action. Any and all sense of discord is but false conclusion about the truth.

You must increasingly come to understand that you have access to the infinite creative power of Law and you must always be aware that in the infinite Presence rests the universal Principle of Perfection. Not only in every way reaffirming Its Presence, you must in every possible way establish within your own consciousness a feeling for It, a sense about It.

Heal the discordant thought and the Principle of Perfection, which always pervades your path, will establish harmony in your experience. Know that It does this immediately, that there is no process of time. Every spiritual mind treatment must incorporate within it the consciousness of completion, of perfection, of fulfillment, in the here and in the now.

There should never be any sense of finality in

PRACTICAL SUGGESTIONS

your self-discovery. No matter how much good you experience today, you should expect more tomorrow. Expectancy always speeds progress; anticipation of better-yet-to-come helps to dissolve the load of disbelief which you now carry with you. You must learn to free your consciousness. Nothing is too good to be true. Harmony is already an ever-present Reality, but as far as you are concerned, It waits to be perceived and only as much good can come to you as you mentally accept.

* * *

The denials used in treatment are for the purpose of removing from consciousness any belief which accepts the idea that there is any manifestation of perfect Spirit which need be diseased. There is neither origin nor cause for disease in pure Spirit. Disease, of itself, is a very factual thing, but not a thing Divinely ordained.

To affirm that the Perfection of God is manifested in you and to deny the negative fact does not mean that you are practicing duality, but that you are coming into a complete comprehension of your unity with God. Very frequently denials are necessary in spiritual mind treatment and you should not hesitate to use them whenever they are necessary.

You must never overlook the fact that spiritual mind treatment is not only a thing of consciousness,

EFFECTIVE PRAYER

but that it is an *active state* of consciousness. It contains definite statements. The treatment moves to a definite end, a specific conclusion that God is all there is and that His Perfection is now manifested. But if, in its process, it is necessary to mentally remove obstructions, then the denial does this.

There is but One Healer. This is the Spirit—God. There is but One Life Principle. This is the action of God in us. There is but One final Law. This is the Law of Mind. There is but One ultimate Impulsion. This Impulsion is Love.

When you array your ideas of the nature of God against the evidence of appearances, you should be certain that the conclusions you reach are positive ones and outweigh all negative ideas which would contradict them. The effectiveness of your treatment lies entirely in your state of consciousness, in whether or not you really are able to perceive more good than evil in any condition or situation.

You should have a calm which transcends the distorted thought and confusion about any condition. You should have a sense of eternal justice which outweighs any belief in, or manifestation of, temporary injustice, and a sense of abundance which completely transmutes a lesser concept of bondage into one of liberty.

It is not enough merely to state your belief or to affirm it as a conviction—this is but the foundation

PRACTICAL SUGGESTIONS

upon which you build your edifice of faith. These are the materials which you mold into the form of definite desire. You must not only know that God is all there is, but you must know that God exists right where the need is—not in the form of the need, but in the form of the answer to the need. The Divine Spirit is the only Actor, the All-in-All, and is now manifesting Itself. Being All-in-All, It has no opposition, competition, or otherness. Firmly being aware of your Oneness with God constitutes a right start in giving a spiritual mind treatment.

In a certain sense it might be said that a treatment is good when you *know* that it is good. In a very definite sense you can have nothing good come out of a treatment unless you first put it into it. From this viewpoint treatment is not a thing of concentration, but is a conscious action. It definitely separates negative thought from positive thought. In an effective treatment you know that there is but One Mind; that this Mind is God, this Mind is good, this Mind is perfect. All movement takes place in this Mind; all action proceeds from this Mind; and nothing moves unless Mind moves it.

The creative action of the Mind of God also resides in the mind of man. There is One Mind used by you and all of us. All have complete access to this Mind, and you are ever manifesting It at the level of your own comprehension or your own interior aware-

EFFECTIVE PRAYER

ness of Life. That any disease, discord, or negation appears to move in or out of a situation is because your mind first conceives such motion. The treatment must have the conviction that it can move it out rather than in.

All the good there is is available to you; not *some* part of it, but *all* of it. It is not only available, it is usable. It is ever-present and inexhaustible. First know that God is all there is, and that God is available. Then that the Divine Law always responds, and that your treatment causes It to respond in such a way as to remove any negative situation and in its place restore harmony.

Your concept of the Perfection of God as being now manifested in your experience is a spiritual power which heals. Treatment is the activity of right ideas asserting themselves through Law. Your constructive use of the Law of Mind, being on a higher plane of consciousness than the state of thought which produced any discord, must therefore erase it, and you must know that it will do so.

* * *

The establishment of your good is brought about through the Law of Mind by the power of your own Divinity. Power exists and the action of this Power is upon your word, or your word acts upon the Power, no one knows which. For all practical intents and

PRACTICAL SUGGESTIONS

purposes, the Power acts upon your word—your spiritual mind treatment—and you establish the word in your own consciousness, with no attempt whatsoever to send it out anywhere.

Never overlook the fact that it is an active consciousness which demonstrates spiritual understanding. While there must be no personal sense of responsibility in healing, you must certainly use your consciousness in such an active way that definite healing may result. To your understanding of the Truth and to your consciousness of Good, you must add an activity of thought. That is, the Law undirected will do nothing, but directed It can do anything and all things. Therefore, in your treatment you give conscious direction to the Law.

There is no way of distributing an undistributed power without first providing a definite channel through which it may flow. There is no possible way of giving an effective prayer unless you direct spiritual Power. This is done definitely as you consciously give direction in your treatment. It is certain that there must be a definite receptivity in your thought if any good results are to follow. Too often people overlook this and merely make abstract statements and so never bring them down to earth .

In such degree as any person can accept harmony instead of discord, he will demonstrate that harmony without having to create it. Never forget that while

EFFECTIVE PRAYER

you can *believe* in that which is not so, you can only *know* that which is really so. Belief that is confused will produce discord, but belief that is centered on a concept of harmony will invariably heal discord. There must be no sense of doubt in your treatment. Treatment should always be calm, poised, definite, and active.

No matter how seemingly impossible any situation may be, or how difficult the appearance of any problem may appear, you must never become discouraged. You must continue to do your work knowing full well that you are dealing with the invisible Divine Presence and Principle—the great Reality back of everything.

It would be impossible for you to do this unless you are firmly convinced that Mind is the only creative agency in the universe and that you have direct and conscious access to Its creativity. Moreover, you must be conscious that through right thought and true statements you are making constructive use of the Law of Mind.

Man's thought *is* the activity of Mind, for Mind without thought or directed consciousness would have no real existence. There can be no existence apart from consciousness, or if there be any existence apart from consciousness then there is no one, no thing, and no intelligence to be aware of such existence. It is evident that without self-awareness there

PRACTICAL SUGGESTIONS

is not only no realization of life, but no life to be realized.

Hence, again you must affirm that Mind in action is Its own Law of fulfillment. When you understand this you will not become discouraged. You will know that if you persist in declaring the truth, the pathway to Reality will be cleared, obstructions will be removed, wrong conditions will be resolved. It follows that you will be happy because you are sure; doubts no longer assail you, fear does not possess you, negation no longer obssesses your thought, and you continue to make your declarations with calm confidence and with Divine assurance.

* * *

You must be careful never to despise your body, certainly never to deny its reality or the reality of any of its organs or functions. There is nothing wrong with the sum total of spiritual Right Ideas that make up your body. Every organ and every function of the human body has a Universal Prototype behind it. They are Ideas in the Mind of God, and perfect Ideas.

You must understand the harmonious arrangement of these Ideas, the unified and harmonious action between them. Your word affirms that the spiritual Idea is now manifested in the flesh—in every organ and function. Most certainly, you never

EFFECTIVE PRAYER

deny that there is a body; you merely affirm that the body is a spiritual Idea right now.

To dwell morbidly on any organ or function of the body is to condemn it, to retard its action, to congest its movement, to impede the circulation through it, and, of course, wherever the circulation is impeded the elimination is also impaired. Every sense of condemnation should be replaced with a sense of praise. You must know that Divine Action is establishing proper circulation, perfect assimilation, and right elimination.

Nothing can adhere to a spiritual Idea except freedom, perfection, and peace, for God is All-in-All, over all, and through all, and in every organ. The functions of the body are not separate from God, but are *within* God. Learn to love all of these functions as being attributes of Spirit and to sense the Divine Universal Harmony underlying all.

The sense of disease and discord is largely in subconscious thought, through which avenue it is transmitted from one person to another or lodged in the general race belief. From this source, through suggestion, it insinuates itself into the consciousness of the individual.

In this way we are all more or less hypnotized from the cradle to the grave, and it is your purpose to free your thought from the bondage of race suggestion. In this case, then, you deal not with disease

PRACTICAL SUGGESTIONS

as a thing in itself, but merely as an experience. It does not belong to you, it is only operating on you.

In your treatment you declare that there is no suggestion, no race belief in this disease which can operate through you; that your spiritual self is perfect, complete, and now dominates your entire being, and that every evidence of discord, fear, doubt, or anxiety is eliminated through the power of your word.

This idea in treatment will have as much power as you *know* it will have. The very fact that the whole performance is mental makes this self-evident. For once you assume that there is such a thing as an effective spiritual mind treatment, that assumption also implies that if the treatment is to be effective nothing can come out of it that is not first put into it since it is a thing of thought.

Really, a treatment is a spiritual entity in which is involved the idea that is to evolve and become a part of your experience. Loose it, let it go, and then have no doubt but that what is *involved* will *evolve*.

* * *

In using spiritual mind treatment for a physical healing of another you must be very careful never to condemn the patient from the standpoint of medicine. From the medical viewpoint the person may have physical suffering because of certain antecedent physical conditions. Or the cause may be a heart con-

EFFECTIVE PRAYER

dition, hypertension, or continuous or excessive mental strain or anxiety. Or he may have the same trouble as a result of over-indulgence, which, according to certain religious beliefs, has been classified as "sin." Or, from the standpoint of a metaphysician, he may have the same trouble as a result of some kind of continued wrong thinking.

Whatever the actual situation may be you must be very careful that you do not attach the disease to the patient. It would be just as wrong to attach it by saying he has thought wrongly as by saying he has acted wrongly, because you must rise not only above wrong physical reactions, but above wrong mental reactions. To say that the man must suffer because of his sin or mistake is no different from saying he must suffer because he strained himself physically, and it is only when the depressing fact of such condemnation is removed that a heart could regain and retain its normal action.

This is something which you must be very careful to watch in all of your prayer work. You must rise above both mistake and consequence to the realm of pure Spirit where there was no mistake, hence no negative consequence. Wholeness has never ceased to be exactly what It is. This is the central realization around which your thought should revolve. There is no place for condemnation in your mind when giving a spiritual mind treatment. Nor should you ever

PRACTICAL SUGGESTIONS

feel that you failed to get good results because of the mistakes which your patient persists in repeating. Your business is to clear up your own thought about the patient and leave him in the hands of that Power which is already Perfect.

* * *

It is entirely possible for anyone, through thought, to condemn the food he eats to such a degree that no matter what he takes into his system it will disagree with him. In this way people actually poison their food through condemnation. While there is no question but that it is a good thing for a person to follow a scientific and sensible diet, he must be very careful in so doing that he does not think too much about the food which he is eating.

In most instances it is fear of food and not the food itself which has a bad effect. Hence you must make a complete mental agreement with it, actually love it for the good it can do you, and never eat unless you are in a peaceful, happy frame of mind. It is a well-known fact that when food is taken into the system while one is agitated or mentally upset, the conditions are such that it will neither digest nor eliminate properly. The whole nervous system is thrown out of gear, a sort of strangulation takes place, and the digestive process is impeded. All of which can be cleared up by creating the proper mental attitude.

EFFECTIVE PRAYER

You should think of food as a spiritual Idea, and realize that spiritual Ideas agree with each other in the one Body of Perfection. They are taken in intelligently, assimilated intelligently, and eliminated intelligently. Every process is already designed by nature to be perfect and you must know that there is nothing in you or in the one whom you are seeking to help which can contradict this perfection.

A good treatment for any kind of physical problem is to declare that all things are now perfect, Life is *already* perfect. Your treatment is the acceptance of this right action of Life. It is this acceptance which enables the healing to take place.

The creative word of good which you use is the Word of God in you, manifesting Divine Power, infinite Wisdom, and perfect Action. Spirit, then, is the Principle of Perfection, Harmony, and Right Action in every aspect of your body. Your word is the cause of elimination, of expulsion to every improper condition. You know that every thought and belief and appearance of the undesired condition is removed. Your word is the enactment of the Law, the activity of the Spirit, the movement of Divine Power through your body.

In your treatment you naturally start with the supposition that Spirit is the only Life, and that this Life is your life. This Perfect Life is your life now. The Law of Mind establishes your recognition of this

PRACTICAL SUGGESTIONS

Perfection as being your immediate experience. All the Power there is is the Power of the Law of Mind —the creativity of Spirit. The only action there is is the action of Mind or Spirit. Hence, in your word rests the ability to remove anything and everything which does not belong to pure Spirit.

You must believe this and definitely state it. Your statements must be specific and you must be conscious of their meaning. Without these two elements of thought, treatment cannot be effective.

* * *

Lack of abundance is not part of the heavenly kingdom. It would be a contradiction of the Divine Nature to think of God as being impoverished. But man is impoverished because he does not see the abundance around him. He does not interpret the universe as a spiritual system; he does not recognize the Spirit as the limitless Source back of all supply.

In declaring that the Spirit is the Source of supply you state an eternal verity. But you must follow this declaration with another declaration that this Source *is now your supply.* The idea you use in your treatment is that Spirit manifests as your supply according to your concept of it. You make the specific statement that you are rightly guided and Divinely protected. You know that every good thing is attracted to you, and that everything that makes life full and

EFFECTIVE PRAYER

complete is now manifest in what you are doing, where you are right now, at this present time, today.

Statements similar to this cause the One Source of Supply to take definite form, and the element of time necessary to produce this form is also a thing of consciousness. For there certainly is neither time nor space without awareness. The action of your treatment is in what you call the present time—it is always "today." Hence, the fulfillment and the completion of life is today. The opportunity is today. The door is open now. The chance for complete self-expression is this moment. This concept is basic in all effective treatment.

* * *

Fear and faith are identical in that the energy used in the one is the same energy as that used in the other, since there is but one final Energy in the universe and this final Energy is the energy of thought. Fear is a positive acceptance that you shall experience that which you dislike. Faith is a positive acceptance that you shall experience that which you do like. But they are identical in their mental action. The only difference is in the direction.

You should be careful not to fight fear too much, but rather, through a sort of flexible imagination, convert fear into faith. Realizing that it is a mental attitude, you can do this very easily. Looking at the

PRACTICAL SUGGESTIONS

thing which you fear and examining the thought of fear which you have about it, convert this thought into one of faith, realizing that the energy of fear converted into faith will produce an effect exactly opposite.

If you will look at the thing you are afraid of until you really understand it, it will no longer have any element of fear for you. You can do this in such degree as you are conscious of being Divinely guided and protected, and state your realization of this in a definite manner.

Love overcomes both hate and fear. However, love does not overcome hate and fear through controversy, argument, or force, but by a subtle power of transformation, transmutation, and sublimation. It is invisible in its essence but apparent through its act. As light overcomes the darkness, as the presence of heat causes the coolness of a room to change until it is warm and comfortable, so the radiant action of love and peace dissipates fear, hate, and confusion.

Love is the victor in every case. Love breaks down the iron bars of thought, shatters the walls of material belief, severs the chain of bondage which thought has imposed, and sets the captive free.

In treatment you should know that love rules your thought and actions, and that you are appreciated by everyone who contacts you. You affirm that fear and hate cannot motivate you, cannot operate through

EFFECTIVE PRAYER

you, cannot do anything to you, do not belong to you, and are no part of you. Allow nothing to enter your consciousness but a sense of peace.

In effective prayer you know that there is no place for anything but good in your life. You know that you do not contradict what you have affirmed; that the statements you have made are the Truth about you, and that they absolutely, positively, immediately, and permanently uproot, cast out, and forever obliterate every negative condition or situation to which they are directed. You never let yourself be misled by appearances or limited by the thinking of others. You accept for yourself only those ideas which you intuitively recognize as being Divine in their source.